Canute's Flute

Written by
Jill Atkins

Illustrated by
Jennie Poh

It was a dull Saturday in June and it had been raining hard all day.

Luke was fed up. He wasn't allowed to play outside with his mates.

His sister, Jude, was fed up too. Her computer was waiting to be fixed.

He jumped off the mule and trotted into the street.

Then he started to play the flute.

The tune was so astonishing that the rain stopped in an instant.

People came out into the street and the sun started to shine.

Canute's flute flashed in the sunshine as he played.

People beamed and clapped in time to the tune.

Soon, the flowers stopped drooping and the prunes even turned back into plums!

Luke and Jude grinned and clapped and tapped their feet.

Ribbons appeared in people's hair. Flowers floated in the air.

Then, all of a sudden, Canute jumped back on his mule and rode off.

Luke didn't feel sad.

"I can still hear the flute," he said with a grin. "Its tune made us all feel so much better."

And off he went to play.